Standing on
My Own Two Feet

by **Faizia Zaman**

Our Lives

No. 3

First published in 1990 by
Friends of the Croydon English Language Scheme Book Group
Reprinted 1995 and 2005

Second edition published in 2010 by
Our Lives Press
Croydon, Surrey
Reprinted 2015

To order copies contact ourlivespress@yahoo.co.uk

cover design by Dimitri Crysto

Contents

Preface to the second edition

Sadly our mother, Faizia Zaman, who wrote Standing on my own Two Feet passed away in 1997. She would have been delighted that a new edition has now been published.

At the end of her book, our mother writes, 'I think my children will be proud of me.' She quotes Arif as saying that her grandchildren will be able to read about her and will know what kind of person she was. This is so true. All five of us are really proud that our mother wrote this book, especially as it is in English, her second language. It leaves us with a wonderful memory of her that we can share with others.

Our mother's dream was that her children should be well educated and be able to stand on their own two feet no matter what comes their way. All five of us are graduate working professionals. We are who we are and where we are thanks to her.

We hope others who have come to settle in England will be inspired by our mother's book to write about their own lives.

Nadeya, Hadeya, Arif, Asif and Kamar Zaman

Dedication

I dedicate this book to all the people who have encouraged me, especially my friends in the Croydon English Language Scheme; and to all the women who, like me, have had to learn to manage on their own in Britain.

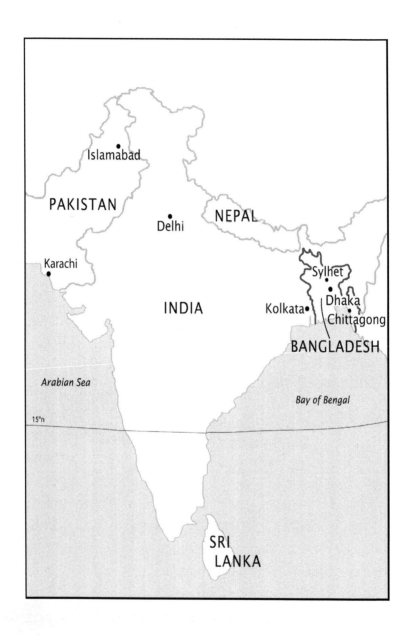

1. Preparations for marriage

It is more than twenty years since I came to Britain. I had come to join my husband. He had been here for six months before I arrived and we had been married for 11 months.

I had spent most of my childhood in my maternal grandfather's big house in the town of Sylhet, Bangladesh. My parents had died when I was seven or eight years old, but I had lots of aunts and uncles to spoil me. My mum and dad had been distantly related and my father's family also lived in or near Sylhet. There were so many people in my grandfather's household that I could not count them – aunties and uncles and cousins, maybe ten or twelve servants and guests as well. The servants and their children lived with us. My aunties and uncles looked after me. I did not have to do a thing except wash my hands at table and even then a servant would help me. My childhood

The house where I grew up

is full of wonderful memories. It was the golden age of my life.

In Bangladesh a young woman is expected to be married soon after she reaches the age of sixteen. Marriages are arranged by the parents, but my parents were no longer alive, so mine was arranged by my father's and my mother's brothers. There is always a go-between in the negotiations. He is usually a friend or a distant relative. The boy's family settles an agreed amount upon the bride, depending on his job and the status of his family. The settlement is usually half in money and half in gold, but sometimes it may include land, a house or even a business.

The settlement is supposed to be given to the wife if she demands it, but no wife ever asks for it. Sometimes the husband's family demands part of the settlement. If there is a divorce this money should be paid to the ex-wife, but there are very few divorces in our country. However, they do sometimes happen, if there has been serious trouble with the in-laws or if they are not happy with their new daughter-in-law; or as sometimes happens, if the girl's parents have pushed her into a marriage against her will. God does not bless divorce but He does give you this way out of an unsuccessful marriage.

A marriage is usually arranged within three weeks. The agreements between the two families and the marriage ceremony all take place within that time. My marriage was arranged within fifteen days. I had never seen Amanuz, my future husband, before our marriage. He had been living in England since 1960 and had made a trip back to Bangladesh especially for the purpose of taking a wife. My cousins went to see him, and his sixteen-year-old sister visited me. She said she liked me; the men of his family discussed the matter and two days later his family made a proposal.

His family pressed for the marriage to take place quickly. My aunt was not happy about it, and my uncles were reluctant to let me go all that way to England. But they were concerned, because my family had already had three proposals for me which they had rejected. Sometimes if a proposal of marriage is rejected, people spread rumours about the girl. So my family finally agreed to accept the proposal. His family had consented to all the conditions laid down in the kabin (the marriage agreement). My settlement was eight borri (one borri equals ten grams of gold).

My family were still uneasy about my going to live so far from home, although it is accepted in our culture that daughters are only guests in their own families, awaiting the day when they go to their real home with their husband's family. When I heard of the forthcoming marriage I became silent. I had been a chatterbox, laughing and shouting. Now I was silent. My uncles were upset; they wondered what they had done to bring about such a change in me. I was quite unprepared for marriage. I knew nothing of life. I was totally numb. I was not frightened, I just could not feel anything.

2. The first years

No one knows what life will be like after marriage. No one knows if it will be good or bad. I had been to college for two years, and had enjoyed studying. I had always been trusted to mix freely with my male cousins. It was a nice life, a nice free life before marriage.

On my wedding day I was ill. I had toothache. I could think only about the pain. When I arrived at my husband's family home he told his mother and sister not to disturb me. He said, "She is not very cheerful because she is ill." They laughed at him and teased him. "You have only just married her," they said, "and you are already so concerned about her!" Bhabi, my brother-in-law's wife, said, "He likes you a lot and that is why he says 'do not disturb her.'" His sister teased me, saying that her daughter had a gold ring which had been intended as a present and that if I had talked to her when she visited me before my marriage, she would have given it to me.

In our culture a husband does not usually talk to his wife about how he feels, but my husband did. He always cared for me. I had the reputation of being quick-tempered. My relatives used to tell me, "When you are married you will never be able to stand it in your father-in-law's house: you are too quick-tempered." And I admit that I was a little quick-tempered. So I thought, "When I get a husband I am going to fight with him." But I was lucky – my husband was a mild, easy-going man. He was so nice that I did not have a reason to fight with him.

We lived for a while at my mother-in-law's house in the village and then we went to stay at my uncle's house in the town of Sylhet, in preparation for my husband's departure to the U.K. You have to go to Sylhet to take the train to Dhaka. We were together for five months, and then he left on his journey back to work in England. I followed six months later to join him.

My husband had a job as a machine operator in a

factory, and was living in a rented place in Hyde, Manchester.

I arrived in Manchester in January 1967. At first I did not know if it was a good place or not. The weather was dark and gloomy. The trees had no leaves. I remember this because where I come from they are always green. The sky is blue and the sun nearly always shines in Bangladesh. When I reached England it was cold and cloudy. Everything looked different. The houses looked different and the people looked different.

Our people are short, slight and also dark. English people look healthy. Their skin is fresh. Visitors to my country when they first see my people think that they look ill. Everybody is much thinner. Constant sunshine dries out the skin and the people tend to look older than their actual age, and many people look sick.

When I first arrived in England I did not want to go out much. I did not want to talk to people on the street. I had learned to speak English at college in Bangladesh though I did not pass my examinations (it was the first time in my life that

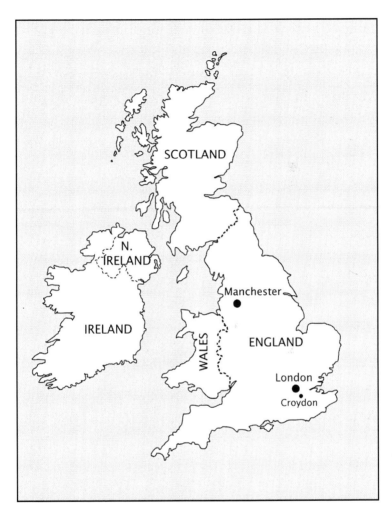

I had failed!). But here I did not understand what people were saying when they spoke to me. How could I respond to their questions? My husband spoke good English. He had been in England since

1960 and had also studied English in college, and studied for a degree. He always told me to try to speak. He said, "You know English. Why don't you talk to them?" I replied that I would feel ashamed if I made mistakes. He said, "It does not matter. It is not your first language. You do not need to feel ashamed if you get something wrong. Try to speak and then gradually you will understand."

My husband worked in the factory for four years. We were saving to make a trip back home. We wanted to show off our two baby sons, Asif and Kamar. We wanted to take them back to Bangladesh to see our relatives.

3. The war

Unfortunately when we arrived there was a lot of unrest in the country. My brother-in-law said, "You've brought trouble with you!" The trouble had been brewing for a long time.

What is now Bangladesh was then the eastern part of Pakistan. East Pakistan had the raw materials but West Pakistan had the factories. West Pakistan sold the manufactured goods and earned the money, while East Pakistan remained poor. The people resented this and wanted independence. Soon after we arrived a revolt broke out and the army from West Pakistan tried to crush it. Soon it was a civil war. Indira Gandhi, Prime Minister of India, supported East Pakistan. Everybody said that India was our Machi's (Auntie's) house; everyone goes to their Machi's house when they need help.

five months in Sylhet we went to stay in a village called Raykelly. Just then the fighting became very intense, and I was stranded there for six months. I was lucky to be there, because I did not myself see anything of the war. But it was a very anxious time, for we heard dreadful stories of what was happening to our relatives in town. There were bombs falling on and around the town; people were very frightened. Soldiers would come and search houses and turn the occupants out. They took money, watches and gold. They stole livestock, goats and chickens. They hit youngsters with their machine guns and carried off young girls. The people were frightened for their lives. They were constantly harassed. A soldier would take a small boy from his mother and taunt her with threats. He would hold a gun to the child's head and say, "I am going to shoot him."

Some soldiers were encamped near my relatives' houses. They never knew when the soldiers would come. They could come in the middle of the night or during the day. There were about fifty members of my family and they would line everyone up, young and old, women and children. The soldiers would ask silly questions. They asked for money.

They asked for watches. They asked for gold. My relatives never knew what would happen next. The soldiers hit them with their guns. The family feared for our girls and thought everyone in the family would be shot.

On one occasion my only brother took a terrible risk. When the soldiers were asking for water, he and our servant ran away for help. They risked their lives for us. If they had been seen they would have been shot. They were determined to try to save our family, and ran to the military police for help.

Soon after we arrived in the village I wanted to send some goods away by ship, so my husband went to Chittagong to put them through customs. After he had left we heard on the radio that the port of Chittagong was on fire. The war had caught my husband. I heard not a word from him. I thought that he must be dead. For six weeks there was no message, no information, nothing. Communications were broken; there were no links between districts. The only news we got was that Chittagong had been destroyed by fire. Later we learnt that this was Indian propaganda to the world to gain support for East Pakistan (Bangladesh).

There was nothing we could do except pray for him. My husband's mother cried all the time. It was a horrible experience for me. My mother-in-law did not speak to me, she just went on crying. She could not look at my face because she was afraid to speak of what could have happened. She took up my two boys in her arms and carried them around. And then one night my husband returned.

When the war quietened down we returned to England. Everyone thought it was best to leave, to escape from the war and possible death.

East Pakistan became the newly independent Bangladesh, and Sheikh Mujeeb was the first President. They called him father of the nation, but later they shot him like a dog. It was so sad.

My husband's cousin, General Osmani, had commanded the Pakistan army's famous Bengal regiment. He was a very strict man and was not well liked. After independence there was an attempt to murder him. A bomb was found in his helicopter. However, he was lucky and escaped. Politics can be a nasty business.

4. In my husband's family

When we returned to England in August 1970, we stayed one night in London with my cousin. I was very pleased to be in London. It seemed very homely because I had some relatives there and I had company. Then we went back to Manchester to stay with my husband's brother. There were lots of people living in the house. We lived as a joint family. I had to draw the hem of my sari, which is called gumta, over my head whenever the men of the family were present. We had to show respect in this way; this is our custom.

It was a difficult time for me because I am the sort of person who does not like to ask anyone's permission to do anything. Now I needed to ask all the time what I could do. My husband was very easy going. He always told me, "Whatever you do, it will be alright." In this way he would give his permission before I even asked for it. When

I asked his advice about living in this country, he said, "I know that you are not bad; you will not do anything which is wrong." I believe I never lost his trust in me.

My husband was the perfect partner for me. I thought that he was the nicest person in his family. Even so, I would sometimes get angry. I did not think I became angry over nothing. For instance, my husband was casual and unconcerned about his appearance. Sometimes he would not shave or comb his hair. I would get so cross that I would start to cry. He would laugh at me and say, "I haven't told you off. Why are you crying?" He was always kind to me, always understanding.

Often when I was angry he would remain silent. Then I would become even angrier. He did not argue with me, he just left me alone. In the early days of our marriage I did not understand all this. Then, when he was in Britain and I was waiting to go and join him, he wrote in a letter to me, "I know that when you lose your temper it is not how you really are. Most of the time you are so nice and kind."

We moved from Manchester to London. My husband worked on the assembly line of Fords at Dagenham and I worked at home, making ladies' handbags. We worked hard and saved in order to buy a business. We were living in the East End in Poplar, in Commercial Road. (There is a joke in Bangladesh that this area round Brick Lane is a cheap place to live!) After a while we ran a café called the Pubali, near the Star of the East pub in Commercial Road. I had a daughter, Hadeya, and another son, Arif. Then we bought a restaurant in Crystal Palace, south London. The following year I had another daughter, Nadeya.

5. Becoming a widow

My husband died in 1980. I was the one who was constantly ill, always going to the doctor with this and that. But lately he had not been feeling quite himself. He was reluctant to go to the doctor but I persuaded him that he should go. He was given some tablets and told that he needed to rest; but he continued feeling under the weather. Further investigations were made and one year after his first visit to the doctor he was told it would be advisable to have an operation. He was reluctant to go into hospital but I begged him to go. Up until this time he had been working in his restaurant. Immediately after the operation he seemed well and we were hopeful. But it did not last. Within six months he was dead. He had had cancer.

His family were a great support to me. My brother-in-law came to the house and arranged the funeral. I did not do anything. This was a big help to me at this time. His wife came and stayed with me for six weeks. All of my brother-in-law's sons came to help me. Other relatives also came to my house.

The funeral was arranged very quickly. My brother-in-law sent my husband's body to Bangladesh. My mother and father-in-law were still alive and they begged me to allow the body to be sent to Bangladesh. We had a small funeral service in a mosque in the East End. I went to look at his face for the last time. Muslim women do not go to funerals; they stay at home to say prayers and to read the Quran. Islam protects women from public grief, recognising that women do the caring in the family and are more emotional.

My husband's body is buried in Sylhet, Bangladesh, in a saint's graveyard. He is buried in a grave with a stone in a very, very special place. His mother went out of her mind with grief. She talked constantly of her beloved son. She did not live long after her son's death. My father-in-law lived to a great age. He was about 108 or 109 when he died. My husband was 48 when he died.

I had a friend who helped me through these difficult

times. We had met sometime before by accident while I was out shopping. I had mistaken her for someone else. I had gone up to her and greeted her, "Asalaam alekum". Then I realised I had made a mistake. She said, "It does not matter. Carry on!" We started to talk and we became friends. She said, "When I come to the market, I will visit you." And she did come to visit me. We became very close friends. She knew of my husband's illness. On the day she came to go with me to visit him in the hospital, I had to tell her that he had died. She cried; I cried. She had recognised the qualities in my husband and had told me, "You have a very nice husband." She always used to say, "I have never seen a man like your husband. He is so polite, so gentle. Don't be angry with him."

One of my nieces, who is just a bit older than me, was also a great comfort to me. She said, "Just now you think you are so helpless, but the day will come when you will be strong, and you will be able to do whatever you want to do. You will stand on your own two feet."

6. Standing on my own two feet

During my husband's illness, the restaurant had run down and I could not devote much time to it as I had five children to care for. After his death things became worse and I was desperate for help and advice. A council worker told me, "If you sell your business, you will get accommodation from the Council." I sold the business for very little money. Then they told me, "You are now intentionally homeless. We cannot help you."

I went back to my social worker, a nice Englishman. He listened to everything. He said, "Don't worry. I will find out for you what you can do." I waited and waited. Nothing happened. I became very anxious.

I have always been grateful to my friend Noorjahan, who persuaded me to go to English classes after the death of my husband. I mentioned my problem at my class. Mrs. Anwar Jamil, a worker with the Croydon English Language Scheme, brought Mrs. Ilyas, an Asian social worker, to my house. She advised me what to do about welfare benefits and how to go about being rehoused. Eventually I was told to go to Taberner House, where Croydon Council offices are. A community worker went with me and I was interviewed by a housing officer. He told me I didn't need anyone to speak for me. He said, "I can understand you and you can understand me. If I think we need some help we can ask." He never knew what he did for my confidence.

The Council phoned me to ask me to go and see them again. They said, "We need a letter from your solicitor when the sale of your business is complete." The solicitor was mystified by this request.

In the end, I was given a letter offering me temporary accommodation. I took the letter to the Citizen's Advice Bureau. They said, "Accept this offer; this is a good chance for you. After four weeks you will not have to leave the house. You are a widow with five under-age children and that gives you the right to be housed."

Then I had another interview with the housing department and I was again asked about my situation. I became angry and said, "I am a widow. I have five children. What would you have done?" "Don't worry, Mrs. Zaman," he said. "We will see that you are all right." I was instructed to pick up the key for a council house at 9 a.m. on the following morning. I picked up not only the key but also all the documents for the house and a letter from the director of housing telling me that they had considered my case and had allocated the house to me.

In the new house, a new period of my life began. A new school for the children, new neighbours, a new English class for me. The class was at the school, and through it I became friends with other women whose children went to the school.

One milestone in my own education was joining the students' committee. I went with two other class members, Shameem and Sultana, and our teacher, Kari Shah, to an evening meeting. I found that I could cope with the English. I asked

Shameem, a widow like myself who lived nearby, if she would go again, but she refused at first because the meetings were held in the evening. Then the meeting time was changed to day time and we both attended regularly.

I found it invaluable to meet students from other classes, and I learned more about the English Language Scheme. I think it helped me with my English because it gave me lots of confidence to talk, to express my opinions and to exchange ideas with other students.

I like the atmosphere in the English Language Scheme. Everyone is very friendly and kind. The teachers and students are like members of the same family. When we come to the classes we speak the same language. Although there are lots of mistakes in the students' English we can understand one another. We can communicate and learn about each other's customs, culture and religion.

With my new-found confidence, I have given two TV interviews, one about the Muslim way of life for a programme called "From Where I Stand", and the other for a programme about parents' choices in schools. I have attended three appeals about my children's schools. I have taken part in teacher training courses in Croydon and have given a talk at a national conference of NATECLA (The National Association for Teaching English and other Community Languages to Adults).

In this country the language is English, so you have to be able to understand and speak the language. Everyone needs to communicate with other people, to express happiness and sadness. I have found out that you have to recognise and develop your own abilities and power if you want to cope with living by yourself in this country. The English Language Scheme has been useful to me in learning how to stand on my own. Now I am teaching in a class myself, and passing on my experience of learning to cope in English.

7. Visiting Bangladesh

In 1986 I went back to Bangladesh. I noticed enormous changes in the way of life. When I was a child we never went to eat out in a restaurant. Now my cousins eat out in Chinese restaurants which are very popular. They like pop music and are interested in dancing. Lots of women have up-to-date hair styles and are interested in fashion. Young girls wear cosmetics and paint their nails. They thought me very old-fashioned because I am not concerned with outward appearances. Even on my wedding day I did not wear nail polish. My great grandmother told me, "On your wedding day you can do whatever you like. God grants you a special day." I wanted everything to be perfect for my wedding day: I wanted to complete my prayers. Nail polish is a lot of bother to put on and you have to clean it off before you can pray.

In Bangladesh today even the rickshaw drivers

can understand some English. Everyone hears English on television. TV comes into Bangladesh by satellite and news arrives from Britain. People watch lots of films – Dallas, Six Million Dollar Man, The Jewel in the Crown, and many old English films. In Bangladesh TV started in 1962 but only in Dhaka. It was very expensive and only the rich could afford it. When I went back to visit, many more people had a TV, about one family in ten. Neighbours used to arrive to watch in the evenings. Television was on in the evenings from six to ten, and on Sunday mornings from ten till twelve noon. The programmes are improving day by day and they now have colour TV.

I think that television has changed people's view of life. The younger generation watch it and follow the Western world. Un-Islamic things are done openly. Young people have forgotten their origins. I think they should understand that you cannot follow others totally. In this country I notice that young people sometimes copy the Eastern world. They wear trousers like pyjamas. The world is changing.

The majority of people from Bangladesh now

living in Britain have come from villages. They are not as well educated as people from Britain. You have to pay for education in Bangladesh. In the villages there are only patshala schools, where one teacher teaches everyone. Private families used to run these schools but now they are half aided by the government. Most primary and secondary schools in the towns are government aided. The teacher is paid by the government but the parents have to pay fees, buy the books, paper and so on. If a village family is poor, the children get schooling only in the patshala, and poor people in town cannot afford to send their children to school.

The hospitals are government financed but there is no medical provision in the villages, and no doctors there. Treatment is free in the towns, but you have to buy the medicines and the food for the sick. Traditionally, families live close together and the families have to look after the old people. It is the duty of the sons, especially the eldest son, to look after the old parents.

Bangladesh is a poor country. Bangladeshis regard the western world as an economic miracle. They have come here looking for work and the chance

A woman inside a rickshaw cannot be seen

to earn a living and with the hope of starting a business. Within a few years they may find there is little possibility of going back. Nobody wants you there. People back home believe that you have lots of money. They call you Londoni, put you in a different category from themselves and do not accept you. The Government too does not accept Londonis. On each visit you have to pay a large sum when you leave Bangladesh. Before the tightening of the immigration laws in Britain, the families of men already in Britain were not so anxious to come here. The women wanted to stay in Bangladesh and thought of Britain as a kind of jail. This is because they have been brought up in purdah and have been taught that they should not go out alone. In Bangladesh this is not such a problem as a woman can travel inside a rickshaw where she will not be seen. Rickshaws are cheap and easily available. The restriction of immigration into Britain has made the Bangladeshi community bring their families here, because they knew if they did not do it before the new law took effect, they would never be allowed to again.

8. My family background

My forebears were landowners. They were given titles by the Emperor of Delhi, the Moghul Emperor. When the British Raj was established, my forebears accepted it. They were unconcerned about power and wealth. They had been unchallenged wealthy landowners for generations. They believed nothing would change. But changes did come when India was granted independence. Laws were passed one after another seizing land from the landowners.

In the old days the landowners had owned village after village, tea garden after tea garden. They collected taxes from the people and in turn paid taxes to the government. My family was well known in Sylhet. Even today when a rickshaw driver asks you "Where do you want to go?" and you reply "To Majmader's house" he will take you straight there.

The family gradually became poorer and poorer. They had never bothered about education. There had always been tutors in the house but mostly no one concerned themselves with learning. They had servants for their every need and money was plentiful. Life was comfortable: there was no incentive to exert their mental faculties.

My father went to Calcutta (now Kolkata) to study and he gained a B.A. You can count on the fingers of one hand the members of my family who have higher education. I will give you an example of the ignorance and complacency which existed in my family.

One of my forefathers was sitting on his chair smoking his hukka. It was evening. There was no electricity and no lights. The jungle was nearby and the foxes started howling. He asked his servant, "Why are they crying?" The servant answered, "It's winter and they have not got anything to keep them warm." My forefather said, "Very well, tell the manager to give them a hundred blankets tomorrow." The next night the same thing happened again. The servant was massaging him. He asked him "Why are they still crying? Did you supply the blankets?" The servant was quick-witted and answered, "Today they are blessing you."

On another occasion one of my ancestors was served a curry which he liked very much. He turned to his wife and asked, "Who made this curry?" She told him that the servant had made it. As a reward he gave that servant many acres of land. The family of that servant are still there and nowadays are richer than us. This family had originally been employed to make our clothes, for there was always a wedding or some such thing for which new clothes were needed. They now own a large tailor's shop.

The Muslim religion says we must be educated and that there should be no distinction in this between boys and girls. It is a religious duty to become educated. Our Prophet said that one drip of ink is holier than the blood of a crusader. But my family only busied themselves with learning Farsi, reading the Quran and reciting English poetry. They were so proud of themselves that they did not concern themselves with the changing world around them.

A few of my father's generation became well educated and worked in government service as Magistrates and Sub Registrars (administrators). They had realised the value of education. The rest of the family sank into financial ruin. They felt bound by family tradition only to take jobs of high status. The British authorities had told them that jobs would be kept open for them and would be theirs once they had matriculated. But most of the family did not care. They had been spoilt by generations of wealth.

9. Bringing up my children in Britain

I did not agree with many of the traditional attitudes in my family and wished to break away. Nowadays a woman can have a career. Some become doctors, lawyers, teachers and even MPs, and even when she is married a woman can carry on working.

Sons have the duty of supporting their parents but there are lots of stupid sons and nothing can be done about that. The family is everything. The Prophet says, "I give my blessings to those who treat their girls affectionately." Our religion says: if you have children you should give them a good education and care for them.

It is my main concern to see that my children are well educated. I would like all my children to gain certificates and degrees. This is my dream and every day I strive for this.

When our children reach adolescence, our religion requires that they should be educated separately. Purdah means not only covering the body but keeping the mind and the soul pure as well. A woman should not look directly into a man's eyes. A man should not look into a woman's eyes. We regard the years between twelve and eighteen as being full of temptation, when boys and girls can easily make mistakes. Boys and girls are not allowed to have relationships before marriage.

It was very important to me to make certain that my children received their education in single sex schools. When my daughter was allocated to a mixed school, I went to my first Appeal Tribunal against the decision. Liz Whiteside from the Croydon Council for Community Relations went with me and we won the right for my daughter, Hadeya, to go to Westwood High School for Girls. In the following year it was the turn of my son, Arif, to move on to a High School. Again he was allocated to a mixed school. I went to two appeals, one at the Stanley Technical College for Boys and another at the Old Town Hall in Croydon. Someone asked me, "Why does your community not provide education?" I lost the appeal. We wrote to my local councillor and spoke to the Speaker of the House of Commons, Bernard Weatherill, who advised me to go to my own Member of Parliament. I went with a friend to the surgery of John Moore, the MP for Croydon Central, the constituency in which I live. He asked me lots of questions. He said that he respected me for sticking to my beliefs, and would try his best for me.

Two weeks later I received a letter from John Moore saying that he would let me know when he heard anything. On the day before the new school year started, I received confirmation of a place for my son at Carshalton High School for Boys. I was panic-stricken, I had only one day to get the uniform and to send in my acceptance. I phoned the Croydon Council for Community Relations and spoke to Ravi Govindia. He rang the school. My son's new form teacher came to visit me with all the details. He told me, "Don't worry, Mrs. Zaman; if you don't have the uniform, send him without uniform. Try to fit him out in a white shirt and dark trousers and a tie."

He has been there for two years now. He is in the top band and competes with two other boys for the top place in the class. He is very happy there and it makes me content.

My two older sons are at college and I only have three children at home now. It is a financial struggle for me to support my children, and as they get older it is becoming more difficult. But I am determined that all my children should have a good education.

10. Telling my story

People ask me, "How did you begin writing your story?"

It started three years ago. One day I went to a book meeting in London. My friend Marion, the English Language Scheme organiser, took a group of us to the meeting. There was a widow, an Indian lady writer – her name was Sharan Jeet Shan – and we heard about how she wrote her book "In my own name". Then Marion told us, Shameem and me, "You could write your story like this." I thought, "I can't write a whole book in English. It's difficult for me." But Marion said, "We can ask you questions, and you can just talk; we can record it on a cassette recorder, and then we can write down what you said." So I agreed.

One morning Susan rang me. Susan is another close friend of mine, and a teacher in the English

Language Scheme. She asked me, "Do you want to write your story? If you do, I can come and ask you questions." We made an appointment and she came to my place. We started to talk, with the cassette player. I talked about so many things; Susan likes to learn about Bangladesh. She came many times, and then she wrote it all down, and brought it to me to read, and to change whatever I wanted.

Now after a long time it is ready. I do not know if people will like it or not. I have written about all the things that have happened to me in the past; but who knows about the future? When my husband was very ill, he said, "I leave you in God's hands." It is because I am in God's hand that I have always found a way out of difficulties.

I think my children are proud of me. My son, Asif, says, "Your grandchildren will read your book and they will find out what kind of a person their grandmother was."